**What Christians
Should Know About...**

Reconciliation

John Dawson

Sovereign World

ISBN: 1 85240 229 6

SOVEREIGN WORLD LIMITED
P.O. Box 777, Tonbridge, Kent TN11 0ZS, England.

Typeset and printed in the UK by Sussex Litho Ltd, Chichester, West Sussex.

Contents

1

Hatred's End

Reconciliation takes place when you and I begin to enjoy intimate fellowship with our previous enemies, people who have tempted us to bitterness by hurting us. This is a miracle made possible by the cross of Jesus Christ. At the cross, mercy triumphed over justice. At the cross, a mighty flood of reconciling grace was released into the earth. At the cross, we ourselves were recipients of such mercy that it changed the way we viewed those who had sinned against us. Jesus healed our broken hearts through reconciling us to the Heavenly Father, but He also commissions us to the ministry of reconciliation in the world in which we live. We begin this ministry by simply telling our own story of failure and forgiveness to all who will listen.

The gospel, Greek for "good news", is simply this: everybody has sinned. Sin is that which violates relationships, the selfish acts that separate us from one another and from God. However an atonement for sin has been mediated through Jesus' sinless life, unjust death and triumphant resurrection. Because of Christ, we can be reconciled to our Creator and to each other.

Who Do You Hate?

Every Christian encounters the temptation to hate at some time or another. You may be a mother who has witnessed the suffering of your beloved daughter at the hands of an abusive son-in-law. You may have lost everything through betrayal in a business transaction or been fired unjustly. You may be a member of a people-group who has experienced rejection and injustice for generations. It is impossible to have lived without being hurt by something. We know hatred is wrong, but how do we come out of it?

Paradoxically people sometimes suffer an even greater temptation to hate **after** their salvation experience. How can that be? It is because the unregenerated heart is often protected by walls of cynicism. Many people outside of Christ have lowered their expectations of their fellow man to the point where they expect to be hard done by and put upon. When injustices occur there is no shattering disappointment; it simply confirms that person's view of life. On the other hand, followers of Jesus have been flooded with hope at the moment of their new birth. They are transferred from the kingdom of darkness to the Kingdom of God's dear Son and their expectations change completely. Their standard is now love and its attributes. They begin to imitate Jesus and to anticipate Christlike behavior from those who claim to follow Him. This is why the wounds received in a church or Christian organization cut so deeply. Disappointment comes from failed expectations and the temptation to bitterness and alienation can be intense, particularly if it is somebody in leadership who has failed us.

What Can We Do About It?

Have you ever attempted reconciliation while the painful memories still tormented you? There will be no reconciliation with anybody until we bring our broken hearts to Jesus first. Healing begins when we honestly confront the past. Before we can even contemplate forgiveness, we need to face what really happened and bring it to the foot of the cross.

I have a Welsh friend named Rhiannon Lloyd who holds trauma recovery classes for both Hutu and Tutsi survivors of the Rwanda genocide. If you were in her shoes, what would you say to these devastated people? Many have experienced rape or maiming or witnessed the murder of their family members.

This is what she does: in the shelter of a church house they meet for three days. Dr. Lloyd first persuades her grieving flock to write down on a piece of paper the worst experience that they had.

When the awful facts have been confronted in this way, she has them come together in small groups to tell each other their stories. This is often the first trembling step towards trusting other people again.

Finally the terrible atrocities are listed on a large sheet of paper for all to see and the group is asked "What does God feel about this?" She then draws a big red cross through the list of hurts, symbolizing the cross of Christ. "This is the only place we can bring our sorrows," she tells them. "This is one of the reasons Jesus came to earth; not only to take upon Himself our sins, but also the sin of those who have sinned against us. Stand and tell God of the pain in your heart," she tells them. "What you saw, what it did to you. If you're angry, tell Him. If strong emotion comes, don't hold it back, because God will be weeping with you."

At first there is silence, but sobbing and wailing soon overcomes the cultural reserve of the Rwandans as people pour out their grief, anger and hopelessness before the crucified Christ. A long time later, when quiet returns, they sing softly the old chorus "What a friend we have in Jesus, all our sins and griefs to bear." Eventually Rhiannon brings in a big, rough wooden cross and positions it on the floor with a pile of nails. One at a time, believers begin to slip forward and taking their tear-stained piece of paper with its record of horrors, they kneel and nail it to the cross of Jesus. All afternoon the hammer pounds, echoing the agony of Golgatha, a reminder of Jesus' complete identification with our sufferings.

On the third day an amazing thing happens. People begin to testify that in the midst of genocide, God was at work in the darkness. They talk of heroes, Christian reconcilers who were the first to die. Anger at God begins to turn to empathy for God as believers contemplate His heartbreak over the way we humans treat one another.

With grief now resting lighter upon many, talk of forgiveness begins to emerge. Jesus is seen, not only as the innocent and suffering Lamb of God, but also the resurrected and righteous Judge who will uncompromisingly administer justice. Even now His hand of vengeance is stretched out toward the wicked, the very persons haunting the memory of survivors.

"If they repent, is it all right with you if God forgives them?" Rhiannon asks. Each person contemplates this question, weighing their own testimony of cleansing against their grief, many finally concluding that if God forgave them, they must eventually forgive others. Truly this is "beauty for ashes", the promise of God. (Isaiah 61:1-4)

Healing the Land

Finally Rhiannon tells them a personal story. "I come from a nation where two tribes have hurt each other," she says. "One day I was in a prayer meeting when an English Christian knelt at my feet. 'We have often made the Welsh our servants.' she said. 'Please forgive us.' And she proceeded to wash my feet. A deep healing took place in my heart that day because of the humility of one person who chose to identify with the sins of her people against my people."

Rhiannon's simple story contains a key. The key to the ancient gates that isolate peoples and elements of society from one another. She has given a wisdom gift to Hutu and Tutsi as they struggle to live together in the same land.

You see, Jesus didn't tell us to apply the cross to the other person, but to ourselves. This is what gives us power to be reconcilers. It is a mystery revealed in the cross of Christ. Each believer must take up the cross and apply it to their own identity. Even now God is looking for people like Rhiannon's humble English friend. He's looking for those who will express the humility of Christ and bring healing to the nations.

Rhiannon acts upon this truth. She does one more thing. As a white person surrounded by Africans, she takes a position of complete identification[1] with Europeans. She cannot represent Europeans in any official way, let alone confess the sins of others, but she realizes that there are no "generic" Christians. We all come from somewhere and it is obvious to the Africans that she is from one of the European peoples that long held power in Africa.

Rhiannon knows that her very appearance reminds many Africans of rejection and unjust dominance, but instead of disclaiming all association with the colonial past by such statements as, "I'm not from Belgium," or "It was all in a past generation," or " My people have been oppressed too," she volunteers to stand in the gap as an intercessor. The Bible reveals that God is looking for such people. Not just people who will stand in the gap before Him, but people who will repair the breaches in human relationships.

God does not put guilt on the intercessor. We are not individually guilty for what our group did or our parents did, but He is waiting for the "royal priesthood", which is the redeemed in Christ, to openly confess the truth of a matter before Him and before people, just as the ancient Hebrew priests once did over the sins of Israel. You see, it is very difficult to forgive if you have never heard an open acknowledgement of the injustices that wounded you or your people. On the other hand, such grace for forgiveness is released when we are asked for forgiveness by those who identify themselves in some way with the identity of those who contributed to our suffering.

---

[1] Identification: As used in this sense, signifies the act of consciously including oneself within an identifiable category of human being.

2

Reconciliation
With God

For the believer the works of reconciliation begin with God, not the human subject of any conflict. We are called first to be worshippers and intercessors standing in the presence of the Creator. Human to human reconciliation is a byproduct of that primary relationship.

The followers of Christ have an incomparable power to heal relationships because of their unique freedom to be completely honest. All the religions and ideologies deal with guilt, either personal or corporate, by transferring blame to nature, matter or society. Whatever it purports to be on the surface, an ideology's deepest appeal to the human heart is through its guilt transferral mechanism, some naturalistic or religious theory that employs the intellect in justifying an individual's sinful choices.

In contrast to this, the followers of Jesus find that it is the things openly acknowledged and confessed that are cleansed and forgiven while the sins we have covered up are sure to bring down judgment. Reconciliation with God begins with honesty, thus teaching us that reconciliation in human relationships must begin the same way.

In the Bible the redeemed of all nations are called *"a royal priesthood, a holy nation, a people for God's own possession..."* (I Peter 2:9). What does that mean? For too long we have glossed over this title as though it was merely a term of endearment rather than a job description.

In fact this New Testament passage has profound implications because it suggests that the responsibilities once taken by the Hebrew priests are in some way transferred to us even though the atoning work of Christ on the cross is complete.

The New Testament emphasizes the salvation of individuals but continues to affirm that God is dealing with corporate entities such as our nation, people group or even a sub-structure within society. Consider the words of Jesus in Matthew 23:29-32 *"Woe to you, scribes and Pharisees, hypocrites! For you build the tombs of the prophets and adorn the monuments of the righteous, and say 'If we had been living in the days of our fathers, we would not have been partners with them in shedding the blood of the prophets.' Consequently you bear witness against yourselves that you are sons of those who murdered the prophets. Fill up then the measure of the guilt of your fathers."*

Here we see specific reference to the judgment of God on a multigenerational vocational cast, the stewards of the temple. Jesus teaches that both their corporate and personal guilt are unresolved before God because of lack of repentance.

Remitting Sin

Are we remitting the sins of our nation or group as modern intercessors? Or have we neglected the example of the great intercessors of the Bible?

> *Let Thine ear now be attentive and Thine eyes open to hear the prayer of Thy servant which I am praying before Thee now, day and night on behalf of the sons of Israel Thy servants, confessing the sins of the sons of Israel which we have sinned against Thee; I and my father's house have sinned .* (Nehemiah 1:6)

There are places in the earth where Christians have been praying for restoration and harvest for generations, yet breakthrough does not come and satanic oppression seems impervious to our declarations of Christ's authority. Intercessors have been taught the importance of unity, purity, intensity and perseverance. Indeed, fervent prayer is ascending in many nations, but it seems that we are missing something or the results would be different.

Here in Los Angeles we are experiencing unprecedented

11

Christian unity, but at times the city resembles the circumstances described in Deuteronomy 28 (curses pronounced upon the nation of Israel if they departed from God). Why?

Much more terrifying than the presence of the adversary is the curse that results when the Lord turns His face away from us. This is what happened to Israel at Ai because of Achan's sin, as we see in Joshua 7:12: *"Therefore the sons of Israel cannot stand before their enemies, they turn their backs before their enemies, for they have become accursed. I will not be with you anymore..."*

Our prime objective therefore, in intercession and spiritual warfare, is not the removal of the enemy but the return of the glory – the restoration of God's needed favor, reconciliation with God. When we encounter a spiritual stronghold, it is not a testimony to the presence of a big demon, but rather to the absence of the glory. Just as nature abhors a vacuum, so it is in the unseen realm. When the glory departs, the demons rush in. We have an enemy that swarms to open wounds and corruption – a characteristic revealed in the name, Beelzebub (Luke 11:15), which means, "lord of the flies." His weapons are accusation and deception, his strongholds are the places of unresolved guilt and the unhealed wounds within the land.

The Need for Intercession

What was true in Nehemiah's day is true today. A repentant church, confessing the sins of the nation before God is that nation's only hope. Abraham Lincoln recognized this truth. During the darkest days of the American Civil War, he summoned the people to: *"... recognize the hand of God in this terrible visitation, to remembrance of our own faults and crimes as a nation and as individuals, to humble ourselves before Him and to pray for His mercy – to pray that we may be spared further punishment, though most justly deserved... it is the duty of nations as well as of men, to own their dependence upon the overruling power of God; to confess their sins and transgressions in humble sorrow, yet with assured hope that genuine repentance will lead to mercy and pardon..."* (President Lincoln gave warning in his proclamation of March 30, 1863).

This was a proclamation to all citizens. To the pagan it says "Repent!" and to the Christian also, but the unredeemed cannot make atonement for the land. The pagan cannot go up into the gap and present the blood of the Lamb. This is the privilege and responsibility of God's people, even if they are just a remnant in the land.

The judgment of God is as real today as it was in ancient Egypt when the plagues came upon that land. Remember when the death angel took the firstborn of man and beast during the last plague? The Jews were not delivered because they were morally superior. Their salvation depended on the sacrifice of a perfect lamb. *"Moreover, they shall take some of the blood and put it on the two doorposts and on the lintel of the houses, ..."* (Exodus 12:7).

Unknowingly the Jewish fathers made the sign of the cross as they placed the blood overhead and side-to-side. God was laying foundations for our human understanding of the atonement. *"And the blood shall be a sign for you On the houses where you live; and when I see the blood I will pass over you, and no plague will befall you to destroy you when I strike the land of Egypt"* (Exodus 12:13).

Through the temple ceremonies, generations of Israelite priests made atonement for the land in this way as they looked forward to the Messiah. We do the same thing as we present the blood, looking back two thousand years to the cross. But what would have happened if one Jewish father decided not to put the blood on the doorposts? That family would have received the full consequence of the plague, awaking the next morning to a dead child. Christians are in the position of that father. There is a perfect lamb, the blood has been shed, but the blood must be applied.

The Missing Key

The question is: what is the role of the Church in presenting the blood? How do we do that? How do we restore God's needed favor and bring healing to the land? We have the promise, but what is the process?

In 1976, II Chronicles 7:14 was written like a banner over the United States, the U.K. and many other nations. Songwriters Jimmy and Carol Owens turned it into a popular Scripture chorus and the theme of large worship and prayer gatherings. Many of today's prayer movements had their beginnings at that time and it seems that every organization quoted this Scripture in its brochure, letterhead or Statement of Purpose. In the United States, half a million people gathered during "Washington for Jesus" with the hope of its promise as the dominant theme:

"If My people, who are called by My name will humble themselves and pray, and seek My face and turn from their wicked ways, then I will hear from heaven, will forgive their sin, and heal their land."

This great effort in the '70s did accomplish much and turned many in the nation to righteousness, but America today is still far from being healed. It is now time to examine this passage again. We must particularly address the question, "What does it really mean for God's people to humble themselves?" First, let us look at the context in which this text was written.

David had died and Solomon inherited the task of building the temple. The work had finally been completed and Solomon received an awesome experience – a personal visit from God. *"Then the Lord appeared to Solomon at night and said to him, **'I have heard your prayer, and have chosen this place for Myself as a house of sacrifice'**"* (II Chronicles 7:12).

This was God's explanation of the purpose of the temple – to be the place where the blood is presented for the purpose of removing guilt. As Paul said, *"... and without shedding of blood there is no forgiveness"* (Hebrews 9:22).

Then God briefly refers to the curses in Deuteronomy 28: *"When I shut up the heaven and there is no rain, or command the locusts to devour the land, or send pestilence among my people..."* (II Chronicles 7:13). After this, the conditions of heart and attitudes that God wanted to see in the people are mentioned because a ritualistic presentation of the blood by an unrepentant people would not make atonement for the land. God was looking for genuine responses on the part of His people before the land would be healed.

Let's look at these conditions one at a time. *"If My people who are called by My name..."* He is addressing us, not the pagans. Our nation will be cursed, or blessed, according to the obedience or disobedience of the Church.

"... will humble themselves..." this is the statement we understand least and neglect the most. We understand what it means to pray and to repent, but what does it really mean for us to humble ourselves?

As an exercise, take a minute and see if you can feel immensely humble right now. It does not work that way, does it? Humility has to be more than a pious mood – it is an attitude expressed through dynamic action. The most obvious action associated with humility is thanksgiving, which is to acknowledge our debt to another. When God sees a grateful heart he reads humility, but there is an even more radical action – an action that brings both cleansing and healing – the act of confession.

> *If we confess our sins He is faithful and just to forgive us our sins and to cleanse us from all unrighteousness.* (I John 1:9)

> *Confess your faults one to another that you may be healed.*
> (James 5:16)

Cleansing and Healing

The Scriptures also teach that the act of confession is as powerful in effecting the cleansing and healing of nations as it is in individuals. This is seen especially in the "restoration books" such as Nehemiah and Ezra, where Israel had fallen to its lowest condition as a nation, but humility and repentance began the process of restoration.

In many ways America has become worse since 1976, particularly the alienation between genders, races and political ideologies. At "Washington for Jesus", the huge gathering on the mall, we briefly made mention of our national sins, but was it enough? Have we really ever practised in America the identificational repentance exemplified by the priests and prophets of the Bible? This is the question now troubling many American intercessors.

In 1997 approximately 1.4 million Christian men again gathered in Washington DC. This time repentance was expressed at a much deeper level because it was much more specific. We had begun to understand God's view of the sins of idolatry and injustice and the degree to which we, the Church, have sinned against God and each other.

I personally experienced a new level of conviction and brokenness. Being asked to help lead a section on racial reconciliation, what came pouring out of my heart was a white man's confession. The speaker before me, an African American, had just testified to the pain experienced by his people. I found myself kneeling before the vast crowd speaking an unrehearsed prayer of repentance before God: "Lord I confess that we are an arrogant people, that we have deeply wounded African American and Jewish and Native American and Hispanic people in the story of this land. Even unconsciously, the way we stand, the way we talk, the way we think about ourselves projects an incredible sense of superiority about everything. We don't even see it... We've been a greedy people. Because of our love of money, we have broken treaties with Native Americans. Hundreds of treaties. Our forefathers enslaved Africans, rejected Asians, exploited Hispanics, excluded Jews. And Lord, these were sins in the Church, not just in the nation. We aplogize to you Lord. In our place of authority and privilege we have misrepresented your character and nature. We have abused power. We who haven't believed we're racists, yet we're all racists. We humble ourselves, Lord. This is your nation, not our nation. Lord have mercy upon us. Lord have mercy upon us." Hundreds of thousands of European Americans knelt with me on the Mall and in auditoriums around America linked to the event by satellite.

Is it possible that evangelical Christians have devalued confession because of our roots? There was great abuse of the confessional prior to the Reformation. Are we in a state of reaction? What is really biblical in regard to this important truth?

16

What is the posture of the interceding Church in the midst of nations polluted with blood and blinded by self-sufficiency?

Stark Honesty

I was once visited by a businessman who had been listening to my teachings by cassette tape. "I don't know how you can have such hope," he said. "This culture is rotten to the core." How would you answer him? It's true, wickedness is woven into the fabric of our culture. Is there hope?

The gospel reveals a message of faith, hope and love. Faith is receiving the knowledge of the Father's ability and character. Hope is the expectation of His goodness, and love is the experience of intimate affection, the embrace of the Father, His grace poured out. However, the promise of the gospel is only realized as human hearts identify with Christ, our great intercessor, in His ongoing labor of prayer. That is why the intercessor weeps. Like Jesus, he or she identifies with both God and humanity.

The great intercessors of the Bible all approached God with a genuine sense of shame and embarrassment. They did not come into God's presence in order to cover up sin but to agree with His assessment of it, to face with stark honesty the wickedness of the culture around them. The prophet Jeremiah is a good example of this, as he stated:

> "...For they proceed from evil to evil, and they do not know Me, declares the Lord. Everyone take heed to his neighbor, And do not trust any brother; For every brother will utterly supplant, And every neighbor will walk with slanderers. Everyone will deceive his neighbor, And will not speak the truth; They have taught their tongue to speak lies, And weary themselves to commit iniquity." (Jeremiah 9:3-5)

Intercession is not an escape from reality. Our communication with God must be rooted in the truth – the eternal truth of His holy standards and the awful truth about our society as God sees

17

it. The intercessor experiences the broken heart of God through the indwelling presence of the Holy Spirit. The intercessor also identifies with the sin of the people, because the intercessor has personally contributed to God's grief.

Our God is a God of patience and compassion beyond human comprehension. His grief and torment because of the sin of His people is also poured out through the prophecy of Jeremiah.

> *"Why have they provoked Me to anger with their carved images, And with foreign idols?... For the hurt of the daughter of my people I am hurt. I am mourning... Oh, that my head were waters, And my eyes a fountain of tears that I might weep day and night for the slain daughter of my people!"* (Jeremiah 8:19; 21; 9:1)

The Paradox of Identification

In responding to the broken heart of God, we need to identify with the sins of the nation in personal and corporate repentance. Even though Nehemiah was apparently a very righteous man and innocent of the specific sins that the nation of Israel had committed, when he prayed for the restoration of Israel he prayed as a member of the guilty nation, identifying with their sins, saying, *"I and my father's house have sinned"* (Nehemiah 1:6-7). Ezra went even further when he said, *"Oh my God: I am too ashamed and humiliated to lift up my face to You, my God; for our iniquities have risen higher than our heads, and our guilt has grown up to the heavens"* (Ezra 9:6).

Both Ezra and Nehemiah were righteous men, but they so identified with the people that they were interceding for that they considered themselves guilty with them. You may be a righteous person who is not involved in any direct way with the vices present in your nation, but there is no temptation which is not common to humanity (I Corinthians 10:13). We can all identify with the roots of any given sin, *"For all have sinned and fall short of the glory of God"* (Romans 3:23).

Consider, for example, the shedding of innocent blood in the act of abortion. You may never have participated in an abortion, but all of us have been guilty of the root sins which give place to such an activity. I can think of five common roots that lead to abortion: lust, the love of comfort, the love of money, rejection and unbelief.

- Lust: it is often the context for irresponsible conception.
- The love of comfort: the decision to abort is often made simply to avoid the discomfort of pregnancy.
- The love of money: it is a choice often made to avoid financial sacrifice even though a human life is at stake.
- Rejection: in her fear of rejection by society or boyfriend, a woman's solution is in fact to reject – the child in her womb.
- Unbelief: we discount the existence of a just God who will surely honor a difficult but righteous decision. The voice of unbelief concludes, "If I have this baby, it will ruin my whole life!"

These are struggles common to us all and illustrate the need for honest identification with the sins of our nation when we stand before God asking for His mercy. Nehemiah and the families with him assembled themselves before the Lord with fasting, in sackcloth and with dust on their heads. Though they were just a remnant, they completely identified with their nation and its history. *"Then those of Israelite lineage separated themselves from all foreigners; and they stood and confessed their sins and the iniquities of their fathers"* (Nehemiah 9:2).

When we ask for God's mercy on others, we should never say "How could they do such a thing?" We know exactly how they could do it, because the potential for the worst evil lies within each one of us, apart from God's saving grace and the life of Christ within us. *"I find then the principle that evil is present in me, the one who wishes to do good,"* Paul said in Romans 7:21.

It's Personal

God often gives me an objective in prayer and fills me with faith for an answer. I may be praying for a needy neighbor or praying for a nation. As I struggle in prayer for others to be released from spiritual bondage, the Lord begins to reveal the depravity of my own heart in order to bring me into the place where I can intercede with humility and honesty. God cannot use an unclean vessel in the place of intercession: *"If I regard iniquity in my heart, the Lord will not hear"* (Psalm 66:18).

First comes cleansing, then comes power, as Joshua related: *"Sanctify yourselves, for tomorrow the Lord will do wonders among you"* (Joshua 3:5). We cleanse ourselves by repentance, which is to humble ourselves and acknowledge our sin, then we go to the cross for the forgiveness and power to turn away from the sin. The Scriptures teach repeatedly that we cannot do this for ourselves only, but also for the entities with which we identify. This is one of the great lessons of the lives of Joseph, Moses, David, Ezra, Nehemiah, Daniel, Jeremiah, and most of all – our Lord Jesus Himself. Is this not what Jesus did for us on the cross? To bear our sins He had to become one of us.

For true intercession we must gain a place where we trust God, and God trusts us. For this reason we should continually pray as David did, *"Search me O God, and know my heart, try me and know my thoughts; and see if there is any wicked way in me, and lead me in the way everlasting"* (Psalm 139:23-24). Our trust of God comes through the cross and the unfathomable love that He demonstrated for us there. His trust for us also comes through the cross, as He sees us abiding in His Son by taking up our crosses every day to follow Him. We do not take up our crosses in order to crucify our own flesh because we were already *"crucified with Him"* (Galatians 2:20). We take up our crosses like Him, and through Him, to lay down our lives for others. This is the essence of intercession.

When God has tested us and found a heart totally dedicated to His purpose, then He gives the promise of access to His power. *"If you abide in Me, and My words abide in you, you will ask what you desire, and it shall be done for you"* (John 15:7). At this point our prayers become effective in releasing the power that changes things, as James explained, *"Confess your trespasses to one another, and pray for one another, that you may be healed.*

The effective, fervent prayer of a righteous man avails much" (James 5:16).

"Take Over, Jesus…"

The Holy Spirit prays through us as the divine **intercessor** *"with groanings which cannot be uttered"* (Romans 8:26-27), but limits Himself to exercising an authority proportionate to the degree of yielding of the human vessel. It is my own testimony that the victories of my life have always come in the midst of repentance and confession.

When I come back to the cross I experience again cleansing and forgiveness. The consequences of my sin have fallen upon the Lamb that was slain. The blood is again sprinkled on the doorposts of my heart. Instead of perfecting righteousness in me, He who is righteous is standing up within me and beginning to live His life. Jesus is the only person who can truly live the Christian life. I acknowledge again my total dependence on Him.

We are by nature incomplete. Human beings by definition are the dwelling place of God. God has created us as a vessel for His own being. In a sense, we cannot be fully human apart from Him. Jesus does not dispense His attributes to us as we need them; He does not give us some love – He **is** love. His life unleashed within us is the source of all victory and blessing. He is everything that I am not. He is consistently loving, completely honest and quick to forgive. My only hope is to acknowledge consciously my desperate need of Him. "Jesus, live Your life through me" has become my daily prayer.

My biggest problem is not demons; I am my biggest problem. It is only when God has cleansed my own wicked heart that participation in the redeeming work of intercession/reconciliation becomes possible. It is then that the power to change history is released through prayer. *"Elijah was a man with a nature like ours, and he prayed earnestly that it would not rain; and it did not rain on the land for three years and six months: And he prayed again, and the heaven gave rain, and the earth produced its fruit"* (James 5:17-18).

As we stand in the gap for those the Lord has called us to stand for, He is giving us the most wonderful opportunity to abide in Him and participate with *"Him who always lives to make intercession"* (Hebrews 7:25). To abide in the Light, we must allow the Holy Spirit to shine the bright light of truth into the inner rooms of our souls. We must run from the religious deceit that would seduce us into believing that we are superior to any person. It is only by the blood of the Lamb and the power of the Spirit that we stand free from the chains of guilt and the sentence of death. As Isaiah exclaimed when he came into the presence of the Lord, *"Woe is me for I am undone! Because I am a man of unclean lips, And I dwell in the midst of a people of unclean lips; For my eyes have seen the King the Lord of hosts"* (Isaiah 6:5).

What does it mean to be unclean? All sin involves the violation of relationships. Sin is first the violation of our relationship with God, but it is also the violation of relationships between individuals, and between people-groups, such as blacks and whites, Catholics and Protestants, or males and females. Spiritual strongholds are places of unresolved guilt and wounding that have been infested by opportunistic demons. Again, our primary objective as intercessors is not to break the power of demons, but to restore the glory of God.

Why Me?

If the people of your nation have broken covenants with God and other nations and violated relationships with one another, the path to reconciliation could begin with your act of confession. The greatest wounds in human history, the greatest injustices, have not happened through the acts of some individual perpetrator. Rather they have happened through the institutions, systems, philosophies, cultures, religions and governments of humankind. Because of this, we are tempted to absolve ourselves of all individual responsibility. However, God looks for individuals to "stand in the gap" just as He spoke through Ezekiel:

And I searched for a man among them who should build up

the wall and stand in the gap before Me for the land, that I
should not destroy it; but I found no one.   (Ezekiel 22:30)

This is a most amazing statement made by the Lord after the land of Israel had been destroyed by the Chaldeans. Could this great tragedy have been avoided by a single man who would build the wall and stand in the gap before the Lord for the land? That is certainly the implication. This gap is the breach between God and people that is created by transgression. The Lord Himself looked for a person who would stand in that breach for the land, but He could not find anyone.

Let us take this more personally. How many marriages have been destroyed because there was no one who would stand before the Lord for them? How many race riots have erupted because there was no one to stand in the breach for them? How many churches have perished because no one would so identify with the breach so as to stand in it before the Lord for that congregation? We might think, "well the Lord could do this for Himself," but it is fundamental to His plan that everything He will do here He will do through us – He is always looking for a man or woman to work through, even in His ministry of intercession.

Unless someone identifies themselves with corporate entities such as the nation of our citizenship or the subculture of our ancestors, the act of honest confession will never take place. This leaves us in a world of injury and offence in which no corporate sin is ever acknowledged, reconciliation never begins, and old hatreds deepen.

The followers of Jesus are to step into this impasse as agents of healing. Within our ranks are representatives of every category of humanity. In fact, our identity (gender, race, nationality, language, etc.) is one of the greatest intercessory tools God has given us; it's not just an accidental result of family biology or heritage. Trembling in our heavenly Father's presence we see clearly the sins of humankind. It is not our job to cover up these sins, but to live out the biblical practice of identificational repentance, a neglected truth that opens the floodgates of revival and brings healing to the nations.

3

Peacemaking in the New Century

Today we live in a wounded world. The Cold War is over. The great transnational ideologies have either failed or proved to be weak. Communism has collapsed, and even the fanatical fervor of Islamic fundamentalism has been unable to bring Islamic regions and peoples together.

Into the sociopolitical vacuum has rushed the much older claims of nationality, language, religious schism and tribal identity. The old hatreds are back with a vengeance. Ancient fault lines that were briefly covered over are once again exposed.

Racial strife among the immigrants of New World cities; people-group wars in the post colonial states of Africa; ethno-religious convulsions in east Europe: these are all symptoms of the foundational conflicts that this generation receives as a legacy of the past.

Racial conflict in particular has dramatically impacted my personal life. I am a white man. I have lived for the past twenty years in the African American community in the United States. My neighborhood became famous world-wide as the place where officers of the Los Angeles police department were caught on video mercilessly beating a black man named Rodney King. Following their acquittal the city erupted. Fifty-nine people died in the rioting and more than 5,000 buildings were damaged or destroyed. Mr. King was later quoted in banner headlines around the world asking the desperate question, "Can't we all get along?" Mr. King's question hangs over us still… The answer, of course, is no.

Business as usual for the human heart is envy, fear and contention and God will ultimately thwart any attempt to usurp the place of His own kingdom through solutions based on a counterfeit system or philosophy. Nation will rise against nation and people against people and the false hope generated by false prophets will be shattered in a series of devastating failures that will culminate in the final failure of the Anti-Christ's one world system.

What an exciting time then to be a believer in Jesus, an intercessor involved in Christ's ministry of reconciliation! We have the answer! (See 2 Corinthians 5:18.) It is only when we are reconciled to God the Father that the "otherness" of another gender, race or culture becomes an attraction rather than a source of insecurity and division.

This is why Jesus gives the ministry of reconciliation to the redeemed in Christ, the living church. The pagans will never succeed as peacemakers. There is only one Prince of Peace.

Even now a wave of repentance is spreading through the world's prayer movements, addressing the foundational sins that have hindered the progress of the gospel for centuries. Much has taken place in the decade of the '90s, starting with the issues that have wounded the New Zealand Maoris, American Indians and other indigenous peoples. I personally have witnessed stadiums filled with weeping Christians where people flooded platforms to confess not only their personal sins but also the sins of their group against other groups.

In May 1995, for example, brokenness, repentance and reconciliation swept the almost 4,000 evangelical leaders from 186 nations meeting in Seoul, South Korea. Leaders from Turkey and Armenia reconciled and embraced one another.

Japanese leaders knelt and asked forgiveness from other Southeast Asians. Such deep repentance, I'm convinced, not only demonstrates God's healing love but also robs Satan of ancient strongholds and triggers the harvest.

As the church of Jesus Christ, our goal, of course, has always been to see people reconciled to God through the gospel. The main hindrance to this end, however, has been us. The world has not been able to "see" Jesus because of the sectarian strife within the body of Christ.

For centuries, this spirit of religious controversy has made us part of the problem. But now, I believe, we are finally becoming part of the answer. The growing wave of repentance over historic sins is leading believers of different denominations, cultures and movements to unprecedented affection and respect for one another. Jesus said that when this kind of unity occurred, the world would believe the Father sent Him (see John 17:21). Ultimately, the world will "see" Jesus when a united church carries the ministry of reconciliation beyond its own walls.

The Wounds of the World

When we study human conflict, we see that Satan's method of getting one group to abuse another is rooted in the hardheaded collision of self-righteous people within each group. Take some truth, polarize the people with different sides of that truth, tempt them to unrighteous judgment and then watch them wound one another with rejection, harsh words, injustice… and so it goes on.

We know that two people can hurt each other through selfish and unjust behavior. It is also possible for a wound to be sustained by a nation or a people within a nation. Animosity and bitterness can fester unresolved for generations.

At a Canadian conference in 1995, Christian delegates from over 40 nations identified 14 general categories of deep-rooted, systemic alienation between peoples and elements of a society, 14 areas in which reconciliation ministry must be applied:

Number 1: Indigenous peoples to immigrant peoples (such as the Aboriginal peoples to European-Australians)

Number 2: Residual antagonisms, when there is justice under the law but wounds continue (for example, between black and white Americans because of the legacy of slavery or the hearing and hearing impaired because of a perception of society's continuing insensitivity)

Number 3: People-group conflicts (such as the Kurds vs. the Turks or the Hutus vs. the Tutsis)

Number 4: Nation-state rivalries (such as the border disputes between Pakistan and India)

Number 5: Independence movements (for example, the

Timorese resistance to Javanese Indonesians as a result of colonialism)

Number 6: Civil wars (as in Bosnia)

Number 7: Alienation between generations (such as a generation returned from war dealing with the counter-cultures of their teenage children)

Number 8: Societal conflicts (for example, Leftist vs. Rightist ideologies on the environment or abortion)

Number 9: Gender-based abuses (such as the forced prostitution of Korean, Chinese and Philippine women by the Japanese military during the 1940's)

Number 10: Industry, trade and labor disputes (such as migrant farm workers vs. agribusiness enterprises)

Number 11: Social-class divisions (such as those caused by the Indian caste system, socialist governing elites, land and business dynasties or aristocratic cultures)

Number 12: Interreligious conflicts (as between Christians and Jews)

Number 13: Inter-Christian conflicts (sectarian divisions)

Number 14: Christianity to peoples (when elements of Christian civilization have misrepresented God's character, putting a stumbling block between those peoples and their Creator; an example is the impact of the Conquistadors on Amerindian peoples)

How do we respond to such deep, gaping, sometimes ancient wounds! The simple answer lies in the humility of Jesus expressed through His body, the church.

A Model For Reconciliation

Although the Judeo-Christian ethos present in many national cultures gives us some basis for hope that reconciliation can occur through governmental or societal entities, I believe that reconciliation ministry is primarily the responsibility of the living church. There is, after all, no substitute for the atonement Jesus provided for sin.

During the great seasons of revival in the past, the church always placed a considerable emphasis on open acknowledgement of sin and called for changed attitudes and just actions. Likewise, today's Christians have the potential to demonstrate a model of reconciliation in the troubled world of the new century.

What is that model? As Christians, we believe in *confession, repentance, reconciliation and restitution.* In the context of healing the wounds of the world, this means:

● **Confession:** Stating the truth; acknowledging the unjust or hurtful actions of myself or my people-group toward other people or categories of people.

● **Repentance:** Turning from unloving to loving actions.

● **Reconciliation:** Expressing and receiving forgiveness and pursuing intimate fellowship with previous enemies.

● **Restitution:** Attempting to restore that which has been damaged or destroyed and seeking justice wherever we have power to act or to influence those in authority to act.

Sometimes we can begin this process by organizing events and ceremonies in which representatives of offending or offended subcultures have an opportunity to express regret or extend forgiveness. An example of this occurred recently when the "Memphis Miracle" ended 88 years of racial segregation among the Pentecostal movements in America.

Of course, in initiating such acts, we recognize that the issues involved are complex. Today's generation has inherited the task of both honoring righteous ancestors and seeking forgiveness for ancestral sins. Honesty dictates that we embrace both the guilt and the grandeur that has attached itself to our various identities.

It is also true that when we are redeemed we become part of the transcendent bride of Christ in which there is neither male nor female, Jew nor Greek (Galations 3:28). But the Bible teaches that we become even more responsible for dealing with the implications of our identity when new life is born in us.

Even though each person stands before God alone and is in no way guilty for the sins of their ancestors or any other group, God is looking for volunteers who will open themselves to experience godly sorrow and confess the sins of the land. This is where reconciliation begins.

God's Momentum

The reconciliation prayer movement seems to have found a God-breathed momentum far beyond human promotion. We are, I believe, in an unusual season of grace, a season of jubilee.

I work with the International Reconciliation Coalition founded in 1990 as a fellowship of Christians attempting to deal with conflict in a Christian way. The IRC has grown rapidly into a worldwide network of like-minded but culturally diverse, praying servants from all streams within God's church. There are intercessors, prophetic ministries, researchers, strategic planners, training ministries and ambassadors of reconciliation who lead the way in public confession, repentance and reconciliation at "solemn assemblies" and other special events.

The IRC has joined forces with intercessors all over the world in organizing various reconciliation initiatives. Our office in Southern California helps with research, training and the networking of experts and materials for the growing number of events, such as the prayer journeys believers are now taking into volatile parts of the world.

A reconciliation initiative is launched when people who trust each other form an alliance around a major reconciliation issue and determine to take action together. The issue may be a perceived trend likely to result in conflict or injustice in the future, a modern group-conflict or antagonism rooted in the events of the 20th century, or a catalytic season of ancient history that still reverberates with ongoing hostility between civilizations, cultures, peoples or institutions. The IRC helps like-minded people find each other and learn from other reconcilers in the network.

At the writing of this book, there are over 60 major initiatives gaining momentum. One of the most significant is the "Reconciliation Walk," coinciding with the 900th anniversary of the Crusades. European intercessors have walked the routes of the Crusades from west to east, carrying proclamations of repentance to Muslim and Jewish communities for the slaughter done in Christ's name.

The response has been mind boggling. Identificational repentance is proving to be the key to opening doors that have been closed for centuries. I don't know why we waited 900 years to repent for the Crusades, but I'm glad the breakthrough among Islamic peoples is coming in our lifetime!

In the United States, people are taking prayer journeys where American Indians were oppressed or massacred. In addition, there are prayer journeys to the historical slave ports of West Africa where black and white Americans weep together, learn together and find an intimacy that has eluded less radical believers.

Radical steps like this are needed to break through the walls of cynicism and ignorance now hedging us in and separating us along ethnic and color lines.

4

Walking It Out

How serious are we about reconciliation? For me, reconciliation has meant moving my Anglo family into the African American community in Los Angeles, fully identifying with its struggles and developing meaningful friendships there. Recently, I sat next to an African American grandmother on an airplane and took the opportunity to ask forgiveness for the sins of my people.

She was cool to me at first but then suddenly opened up, telling me her own great-grandmother was sold at age 8 at the slave auction in Richmond, Virginia. It was not the fact that I write books or address politicians that opened her heart; the conversation changed when she heard that I had lived for 20 years in her community. She saw an authenticity beyond my words.

Your journey as a reconciler may be very different from mine but perhaps no less radical. Abandon yourself to God's purpose, connect to the prayer movements, listen to the Holy Spirit and then take the next step of obedience.

As Christians, it should be our hope that our children will not have to deal with the hatred and alienation that have marked this and previous generations because of satanic strongholds rooted in history. Let us identify the ancient and modern wounds of injustice, pride and prejudice in our world and heal them in a biblical way, without self-righteous accusation or dishonest cover-up.

Mapping the Wounds

The question now confronting us is this. What does the ministry of reconciliation look like? What goals should we set? Start by doing some basic research. Some conflicts are common to nearly all societies. Look at the following list of examples from American culture and begin to think about the issues that affect your nation.

Places of Conflict and Broken Relationship
1) Race to Race (e.g., Native American vs. European American)
2) Class to Class (e.g., Homeless Person vs. Holders of Home Equity)
3) Culture to Culture (e.g., Immigrant vs. Native Born)
4) Gender to Gender (e.g., Working Woman vs. Male Hierarchy)
5) Vocation to Vocation (e.g., Police Departments vs. Civil Rights Advocates)
6) Institution to Institution (e.g., Auto Industry Management vs. Organized Labor)
7) Region to Region (e.g., Westside vs. South Central L.A.)
8) Governed to Government (e.g., College-Age Youth vs. Vietnam Era Government)
9) Religion to Religion (e.g., Muslim vs. Christian)
10) Denomination to Denomination (e.g., Protestant vs. Catholic)
11) Enterprise to Enterprise (e.g., Monopoly vs. Small Business)
12) Ideology to Ideology (e.g., Leftist vs. Rightist Political Parties)
13) Nationality to Nationality (e.g., Americans vs. Cubans)
14) Generation to Generation (e.g., '60s Youth vs. Parents)
15) Family to Family (e.g., Neighbor vs. Neighbor)

This list could be endlessly refined. However, we need something this basic as a guide in order to begin our journey toward national healing. Today's conflicts often have their roots in history so our next priority will be researching the past.

Looking at History with Discernment

Here is a list of key questions to ask when researching your regional or national history:
1) Was there ever the imposition of a new culture or language

through conquest? Were treaties made and broken?

2) What were the religious practices of ancient peoples?
3) Was there a time when a new religion emerged?
4) Under what circumstances did the Gospel first enter the region?
5) Has the national or city government ever disintegrated?
6) What has been the leadership style of past governments?
7) Have there ever been wars that affected your region or city?
   ● wars of conquest
   ● wars of resistance to invasion
   ● civil war
8) Was your city the site of a battle?
9) Why was your city originally settled?
10) Did your nation or your city have a founder? What was his or her dream? Did these people have enemies?
11) As political, economic and religious leaders have emerged, what did they dream for themselves and for the nation? Who were their enemies?
12) What political, economic and religious institutions have dominated the life of the nation? Has there been conflict between them?
13) What has been the experience of immigrants to the region?
14) Have there been any traumatic experiences such as economic collapse, race riots or an earthquake?
15) Has there ever been religious conflict among competing religions or among Christians?
16) What is the history of relationships among the races?
17) What roles have been assigned to males and females in your culture?
18) Are there any common patterns of abuse within families?

Get the Facts

Demographics and trends are also important. Social research publications and the census can be consulted. When you have projected your own list of trends, ask yourself the following questions:

1) Which trends represent the greatest opportunity for the entrance of the Gospel? (For example, an influx of refugees.)
2) Is there an approaching crisis that should become the focus of intense prayer and ministry? (For example, an increase of homelessness or unemployment.)
3) Is there a particular subculture that is manifesting an unusual level of satanic oppression? (For example, a sudden upsurge in teen suicide.)
4) Which subculture is experiencing the greatest degree of spiritual darkness?
5) Which subculture represents the poorest of the poor, the most vulnerable and needy group in the city or region?
6) Are there sociological groups that are actually calling for help? (For example, gang-infested neighborhoods or single mothers.)
7) What is the social issue stirring the greatest community concern in each section of your city or nation? (For example, AIDS, racial tension or property taxes.)

When you have a working knowledge of your region, you will be able to receive revelation from God about a specific strategy for ongoing evangelism and discipleship. Perhaps there is a reconciliation issue that has never been adequately addressed by the followers of Jesus in your area.

Time for Personal Application

In order to explore your potential as a reconciler, fill in the details alongside the list below:

My gender is: _____

My generation is: _____

My native language is _____

Subcultures I identify with are: _____

_____

_____

My class (socioeconomic status) would be seen by others as:

_____

_____

_____

My religious history has been: _____

My religious affiliation now is _____

My family name is: _____

List some of the movements, ideologies, and institutions that have touched your family line as far back as you know:

_____

_____

_____

_____

My location (region – city – suburb – neighborhood) is:

_____

_____

My vocation is: _____

To the people of my extended family I am (i.e., daughter – sister – wife – mother): _____

_____

_____

Referring to the list of common conflicts in society on page 32, look at what you have written and consider the opportunities for identificational repentance created by your unique identity.

Taking Action

Initiative can be taken in two general categories:

1. Catalyst Events

These could be prayer journeys, ceremonies, conferences, reenactments, seminars, reconciliation walks, and solemn assemblies in which reconciliation prayer is featured. These highly intentional events take place within a time frame and are designed to educate ourselves, express repentance before God and break through the walls of ignorance, denial, indifference and hostility that have separated groups of people. Examples range from huge stadium rallies or prayer walks that involve thousands of intercessors and cover a period of years, to ministries like "Aloha Ke Akua", a ministry to local churches in Hawaii that dramatizes the story of the islands through song and story telling and then gives opportunity for reconciliation in Sunday morning services.

2. Bridge-Building Efforts

Catalyst events are important only as a beginning point for reconciliation. Bridge-building efforts will last the rest of our lives and need to be equally intentional.

Most bridge-building efforts fall within the domain of individuals, and their enterprises. There will be collective acts, but individual lifestyle choices are the main thing. Micah 6:6-8 calls us to walk in justice, kindness and humility at all times. When millions of believers quietly act upon their values then we will have truly demonstrated the nature of the Kingdom of God.

Will you hire cross-culturally for your business, not because of government policy but because of your values? Will you cultivate relationship outside your comfort zone? Will you truly listen rather than react when another element of society communicates in a less than gracious way? Will you refrain from judging everybody in a group because of the violations of some members of that group? Will you change a pattern of derogatory speech even if it has been in your family for generations? Having joined a reconciliation alliance will you keep on exploring your potential as a reconciler even after the excitement of initial events is just a memory?

Learning from what others have done

Reconciliation is like courtship. If you make it mechanical you fail, but if it comes from the heart you may succeed. There are no rules except the obvious one: study the other party and respond appropriately.

For this reason I cannot give you a process that applies in all circumstances but I can give you a few examples that demonstrate humility, wisdom and creativity. Perhaps there is a model below that fits the issue closest to your heart.

1. Re-enactments

In Sydney, Australia, united Christians dressed in period costume gathered near the Opera House to remember the violent mass rape of female convicts by male convicts shortly after the arrival of the first fleet. An account was read publicly, Christian men asked forgiveness of their countrywomen and then escorted them ashore with the affection and dignity that they should have experienced the first time. Now, whenever the first story is told the action of Christians in the '90's must be told with it, thus sowing a healing memory into the story of the land.

2. Conciliatory Giving Celebrations

In California, a large suburban church bussed its members over to a struggling African American church. They surrounded the building and surprised the Sunday morning worshipers when a delegation entered the service and presented a $25,000 gift for the building fund.

3. Solemn Assemblies
Common around the world, these events have multiplied alongside the vision for seasons of united prayer and fasting. In Hawaii, 27,000 people gathered in a stadium to worship God and to seek forgiveness and reconciliation over the way elements of society had wounded one another in the story of the Islands. At the end a Japanese leader knelt before the crowd and asked forgiveness for the bombing of Pearl Harbor.

4. Commemorative Ceremonies
Significant dates related to such things as genocidal atrocities are becoming reconciliation events when believers gather to memorialize these painful memories in annual observances. German Christians have led the way.

5. Interactive Citywide Musical Events
'Heal Our Land' a contemporary musical written for united church choirs has toured American cities. Repentance and reconciliation prayer dealing with the wounds of America is featured. Similar events using the arts have emerged in several countries.

6. Justice Action Forums
In New Zealand and Australia Christians are beginning to work with government agencies dealing with injustices in land use and the tribal claims that have been ignored. If there are unjust laws in your nation that perpetuate division, Christians cannot remain silent.

7. Country to Country or Regional Student Exchanges
Christian families are using the student exchange organizations as a way of sending young ambassadors or hosting foreign children in order to build bridges of love between cultures.

8. Appreciation Tours
Korean, Japanese, North American and European Christians moving beyond the traditional tours to the Holy Land and exploring the cultures of other nations in order to empathize with and appreciate the diversity of God's redemptive gifts within the peoples of the world. Reconciliation is a featured part of many of these journeys.

9. Representative Leadership Forums
Around the world Christians are acting as peacemakers by bringing together the leaders of opposing sides. Private Christians have taken surprising initiative in doing the diplomatic work required to get factional leaders or even heads of state to talk to one another.

10. Contextualised Issues Forums
In Durban, South Africa there has been estrangement and fear between Zulu people and Asian Indians stemming from the politically inspired violence that occurred in 1949. In 1997 Christian leaders began to call together the leadership of both communities and healing is beginning to take place. Mapping the wounds of a city quickly leads to the need for forums in which we listen respectfully to the grievances of others.

11. Diversity in Unity Celebrations
Old wounds are eventually put behind us and unity can be celebrated as an accomplished fact. Recently a Los Angeles city councilman visited a block party put on by a neighborhood filled with believers. "If the city was like this block, LA would have no problems," said the amazed politician after observing the obvious harmony between a great diversity of cultures.

12. Receptions, Banquets and other Hospitality-Based Gatherings
Eating together remains one of the most effective ways of bringing together elements of society and Christians with a ministry of hospitality will always be at the forefront of the ministry of reconciliation. This is an activity that begins in the

home and the church dining hall and extends all the way to the convention center.

13. Student Culture Exchange Programs
In post Apartheid South Africa 'African enterprise' takes students from one culture and visits another culture with a view to bring understanding, reduce fear and increase admiration for the 'otherness' of the other people group. In some countries Christian schools are seen as an agent of re-segregation so cross-cultural interaction programs are imperative.

14. Cross-cultural and Denominational Interchurch Hosting
It is increasingly common for pastors to exchange pulpits or for whole congregations to visit one another for combined services and fellowship. Congregations have specialty ministry gifts and the division of labor that God has created becomes evident when believers really begin to explore and 'see' one another in the life of the city.

15. Joining with Feast Days and Cultural Celebrations
Chinese, Mexicans, Filipinos and most other groups with an international Diaspora have special seasons of celebration on the calendar. Events often take place in city parks and are open to all. When an invitation is given to celebrate somebody else's unique gifts and good fortune, Christians should be the first to rejoice with them.

The methods listed above were discovered by united believers in the place of prayer. The Holy Spirit will reveal the perfect plan for you and your team as you also seek God for wisdom.

5

Where
Do I Start?

Become a Worshiper

Jesus Himself should be the focus of the reconciler's heart. Our essential motive in all this is to bring healing and joy to the broken heart of God. We seek the healing of wounds, not because people or cultures deserve healing, but because Jesus deserves to see the reward of the cross, the reconciliation of people to the Father and to each other.

Take the opportunity of confession, with identification, when you find it

Look at the circle of influence God has given you. For instance, through your job. If you have joined the Army, been elected to office, joined the police department or become identified with any other vocation, you are an inheritor of its legacy and have become partly responsible for any unfinished business with God or offended persons.

Don't miss the simple things that stem from your identity – as a father, for instance. A lot of people's hurts center on an absent or dysfunctional father. Sometimes a few humble words can begin a dramatic work of healing, even if there is no evidence of it at the time.

Release forgiveness and refrain from judgment

We must bring our own wounded spirit to God if we are to be

used by Him as reconcilers. All of us have experienced injustice. The obvious temptation of the offended person is to give in to self-pity; a feeling stemming from a deep inner vow that says, "I deserve better than this."

But do we? It's one thing to champion the rights of others; but do we ourselves really deserve better, in an absolute moral sense? I have often wallowed in self-pity but the truth is, the last thing I need is justice.

Justice cuts two ways. What if I really got what I deserve? I'm just another depraved human being with my own history of selfish actions. The fact is, I continue to live and breathe by the mercy of God; and having received mercy, I should extend mercy to others.

The righteousness I now live is by the power of the risen Christ, not the function of an informed intellect driven by the "milk" of human kindness. When I recognize my own desperate need for mercy, the gall of bitterness is more easily removed from my own spirit. When I acknowledge how much I have been forgiven, I am suddenly more able to release forgiveness toward those who have hurt me and mine.

The Bible sets an incredible standard for us in thought and speech. *"[Love] bears all things, believes all things, hopes all things, endures all things"* (1 Corinthians 13:7). Racism and all the other prejudicial attitudes could be eradicated from the intercessor's heart if we simply give the other person, group or race the benefit of the doubt. Leave the judgment to God; refrain from coming to conclusions about the motives behind actions. Do not impute evil intent to any action that could be interpreted two ways. Suspicion and accusation have no place in the heart of the reconciler.

Receive God's gifts of friendship

God organizes and builds His kingdom through gifts of friendship. As you follow principle and live out your particular obedience, God will call others to walk beside you from a diversity of backgrounds. Think again about the people God has put in your life; they're not just associates, God is up to something!

Most of us live in cultures dominated by the ethos of trade. When we meet new people, we unconsciously calculate the advantage we can gain by the relationship. But that is not the way of the Kingdom. Jesus is ready to open our eyes to the beauty and value of the people around us. If we see with His eyes, we will soon follow the natural path from attraction to covenant.

Friendship is an eternal gift. All relationships are tested by difficulty from time to time, but our commitment should be to move toward one another rather than withdraw, to take up an ambition for one another's wholeness, empowerment and release, into the full purpose of God.

Who is present at the edges of your life right now? I know of many white believers who long for a black friend, I know immigrant families who would throw themselves into fellowship with the native-born if shown the least hospitality. Yes there's awkwardness, yes it takes more work than just running with your own crowd, but the rewards are great. Let's go for it!

Join united efforts

The local church, the gathering of believers, is the place where the concepts we have explored can be lived out most dynamically. Congregational life should be the cutting edge of positive change in any society.

We need sermons outlining the biblical basis for racial intermarriage. We need public confession and public reconciliation to take place in our sanctuaries on Sunday morning. We need to give place to the music of every people in our public worship. Let the performing arts flourish and give glory to God. Let the sounds of a huge, diverse world ascend from our gatherings.

Our denominational diversity provides another opportunity. The united Church is beginning to flow together like an irresistible tide. Through events such as March for Jesus, the Church prophetically models the possibility of unity within a diversity on a citywide level. This also helps us, as individual believers, move beyond the tiny postage stamp of our own existence. We need to get involved in the prayer movements, missionary enterprises and mercy ministries of the Body of Christ in our cities. Whatever God has given you to do personally, do it with all your heart.

Volunteer help where your city's pain is most evident. My sister and brother-in-law are part of the network of agencies struggling to overcome AIDS in Los Angeles County. They minister in hospitals and hospices and even nurse patients in their own home until the patients die. An army of similar heroes is already at work in the world. Find people like this, walk beside them and help them.

Attend neighborhood prayer meetings or citywide Concerts of Prayer. If solemn assemblies or reconciliation events are sponsored, be there. You will see nation-changing power released when believers move together in praise, repentance, intercession, spiritual warfare and the proclamation of blessing.

Look around

Be an explorer. Let curiosity carry you far beyond the knowledge you now possess. Seek to understand the times and seasons as Daniel did. Seek to touch, know and celebrate the diversity of your nation. Ignorance is a curse. It will take an informed mind and an enlarged heart to embrace the ambition of God for the people of this generation.

Discern the Body of Christ

What if I was to call you up front in a meeting and ask you a few questions? What if I threw at you the names of five or six denominations and ministries in your town and asked you to explain the redemptive purpose for each one? Could you do it?

We know who is out there, but we mostly know other movements through a negative caricature of what's wrong with them. How they differ from us, the biblical ones. Is there an alternative to these prejudicial stereotypes?

Do you know the value of the movements and ministries in your city? How can you encourage their potential if you remain ignorant of their story? The New Testament Greek word for truth, *aletheia*, means, *"That which must not be forgotten."*

Second Peter 3:1 says, *"Stir up your pure minds by way of remembrance"* (KJV). It is as though the power to remember were an ethical principle, a form of righteous behavior.

When I meet that Salvation Army officer, or that Lutheran cleric, I want to provoke them to renewal by recounting their own heritage, not calling them to imitate mine. Let us give honor to all that is honorable and avoid that contentious spirit that makes absolutes out of what the Bible does not. Every missionary knows there is a great difference between form and meaning; that the cultural interpretation of biblical truth will vary, but the bedrock remains: an understanding of the nature, character and personality of God revealed through Jesus and His work. In addition to the foundational truths held by all the orthodox streams, there are the unique flashes of light shed by each. There is more than a division of labor in the Body of Christ. A division of emphasis also makes possible a wide view of a wide subject: God.

Hold your ground

Satan is terrified by the ministry of reconciliation. We will face opposition, but God's grace is sufficient. Intense spiritual warfare has occurred during the early years of the reconciliation prayer movement, but as I pen these final pages I see victory on every side.

At one point, my darling wife, Julie, was told she had a brain tumor; then the doctor mysteriously changed his mind after prayer and further tests.

On another occasion, my son, David, was walking down the street near our home when he was jumped by five Latino men, forced to the ground and beaten with baseball bats. Fighting free he narrowly escaped abduction. He had just left a barrio birthday party attended by three of his friends, gang members who had turned to Christ just days before. Our van was stolen by local teens and wrecked for the second time. I was threatened by a white supremacist; my son, Paul, was robbed at gunpoint, and these are just the headlines.

The net result of all of this, strangely enough, is that we as a family all feel wonderfully protected. Good things keep happening. *"Out of the eater came something to eat, and out of the strong came something sweet"* (Judges 14:14). It is a biblical truth that we always find some kind of provision in the midst of the enemy's attack.

My son, David, is convinced that God delivered him from a fatal situation (many boys have died in our part of Los Angeles), and at this writing he is an inner city youth pastor ministering to street children, obviously unintimidated by his experiences while growing up.

Go Global

Why not be a part of something big? Remember the wounds of the world we discussed in chapter three? You can be part of the answer.

During the writing of this book I took a prayer journey…

Picture the ancient throne-room of Ferdinand and Isabella in the Alhambra near Grenada in Spain. The palace is buzzing with tourists coming to see where Columbus was commissioned. In walks a large crowd of Christians speaking different languages, including a contingent of Jews wearing yarmulke. The whole atmosphere changes from gaiety to grief. It was here that the expulsion of the Jews from Spain was proclaimed by these same Christian monarchs five hundred years ago. A Catholic priest and a Protestant Spanish pastor lead out in a statement of repentance to the Jews and the throne room is turned into a solemn place of prayer as the intercessors grieve before God over the sins of the church.

Come with me to the hilltop site of the ancient council of Elvira. Here only three hundred years after the Jewish Messiah gave his life for all peoples, the first anti-Semitic decrees were made by Christian leaders. One decree disallowed a Jew to even bless a field, stating that it would amount to a curse. Hear the repentance of the Spanish intercessors and the proclamation of blessing from the messianic rabbis as they look down on the twinkling lights of the cities and villages below. Night is falling, but a spiritual light is rising over Spain as the ancient Hebrew blessing is spoken over the land once again.

Stand in the ancient synagogue in Cordoba. The Jews are weeping. Grieving for the thriving community of their forefathers that is gone completely. Swept out of homes and country by brutal edicts enforced by the sword.

Worst of all, witness the devastation on Jewish faces when they gaze up at the cross of Jesus on the cathedral in Toledo. The high walls of a church still festooned with hundreds of rusted chains and manacles once used to hang Jews as a public example to terrify the large Jewish community into conversion or flight. They cannot stand it. Walking away one Jewish woman sits in the dust, uncaring of the hostile crowd. The rest gather around her sobbing. The Gentile Christians simply hold them. It seems there are no appropriate words. They are still silently embraced as the plaza empties and night falls on the city.

Come with me to the plaza of the great cathedral on Sunday morning. The intercessors are reading with tears the unspeakable edicts of the Inquisition. Christian leaders are repenting – repudiating and revoking the cruel words, finally burning the paper on which they are written.

The crowd parts and a small Spanish boy now stands at the center of the intercessors. He looks forlorn and his hand and arm are heavily bandaged. A Jewish boy in his teens stretches out a hand, and touching the little boy on the head he begins to bless him in the name of Yeshua Ha Mashiach, the Messiah.

These are some of the things I have just witnessed. All I can do is join with the psalmist in saying, *"Lift up your heads, Oh gates, and be lifted up oh ancient doors, that the king of glory may come in"* (Psalm 24:7).

This prayer journey was just the beginning of the "Gates of Iberia" initiative, which in turn is part of a worldwide initiative toward healing the foundational rift between Jew and Gentile in the church, stemming from 140 A.D. A reconciliation movement has been launched in Spain, which while focused on messianic Jews is already having a profound effect on relationships between Catholic and Protestant. There will be many more catalyst events and prayer journeys in Spain and throughout the Spanish and Portuguese speaking world. This will undergird Christian repentance proclamations to the general Jewish communities. You could be part of something like this.

I have described just one event in a global movement that has long since expanded beyond the possibility of human management. Get connected, join an initiative, be a part of the answer to the prayer of Jesus:

> *"I in them and you in me. May they be brought to complete unity to let the world know that you sent me and have loved them even as you have loved me."*   (John 17:23 NIV)

For more information about the International Reconciliation Coalition, contact the international office at:

IRC
P.O. Box 3278
Ventura, CA 93006-3278
Tel (805)642-5327
Fax (805)642-2588
E-Mail: ircio@pacbell.net
Web Page: www.reconcile.org